"Peter and Keith Greer have teamed up to deliver an excellent, practical guide for the budding entrepreneur in your family! This book is essential training for children."

Chuck Bentley, CEO, Crown Financial Ministries

"As an educator, I truly enjoyed reading this gem of a book! *Watching Seeds Grow* uses entrepreneurship to teach children valuable lessons. It's also a wonderful resource on financial literacy for children, families, and educators."

Paula A. Cordeiro, Dean, School of Leadership and Education Sciences, University of San Diego

"Peter and Keith Greer have perfectly framed the important topic of introducing the keys to successful entrepreneurship to the next generation at a young age."

Jeff Rutt, CEO, Keystone Custom Homes, Inc.

"*Watching Seeds Grow* is the best kind of parable: a true story, narrated by father and son, about the power of entrepreneurship. Chock-full of leadership lessons, parenting tips, and highly practical appendices, *Watching Seeds Grow* will serve young and old entrepreneurs alike, with refreshing insights about perseverance, creativity, and innovation that is essential to a flourishing society."

Josh Good, Manager of External Relations, American Enterprise Institute

i

"Our children are wonderfully made! They have amazing ideas, immense capacity, and sincere hearts. The fascinating stories and sound principles inside *Watching Seeds Grow* will inspire children to develop their talents and achieve something remarkable!"

Jason Webb, Entrepreneur and Co-Founder of Soccer Shots Franchising

"In *Watching Seeds Grow*, Keith and Peter combine engaging stories with practical application. I have no doubt this book is going to have an incredible impact on the next generation of entrepreneurs."

Mark Heath, CPA, Partner, McKonly & Asbury, LLP

"*Watching Seeds Grow* has been written in story form to teach us the simplicity of being an entrepreneur. Peter and his son Keith have illustrated a beautiful picture of the satisfaction of becoming a 'contributor' to society rather than simply being a 'consumer.' The power of teaching our children at a young age sets the stage for them for a lifetime."

Anne Beiler, Founder, Auntie Anne's Soft Pretzels

"Two vital skills required to thrive in our economy are financial literacy and sales/marketing. Keith and Peter do an excellent job of explaining these concepts with stories and simple how-to charts. I highly recommend this book for parents and kids alike. Read this book to make an investment in your family's future!"

Scott Heintzelman, Vice President of Finance and Administration, Martin's Famous Pastry Shoppe

"In *Watching Seeds Grow*, Keith and Peter combine two of the most important life concepts, parenting and entrepreneurship, in very simple and practical ways. As a parent who is striving to mentor my children to be job creators rather than job seekers, this guide will serve as a critical tool in my parenting 'toolbox.'"

Eric Munyemana, Executive Director, Rwanda Purpose Driven Ministries/PEACE Plan

"Young Keith Greer's curiosity and inquisitiveness are captured perfectly through *Watching Seeds Grow*. A lesson in life becomes an opportunity in entrepreneurship. Keith and his father, Peter, offer every family reason to believe in our children and our future."

Ron Swantner, Principal, Landisville Primary Center

"Keith and Peter have written a book that appeals to a young reader's curiosity about business and to a parent's desire for practical tools for teaching entrepreneurship, financial literacy, and character. A winning combination for all."

Josh Kwan, Co-Founder of Praxis

Publication, distribution, and fulfillment services provided by CreateSpace, a DBA of On-Demand Publishing, LLC (Scotts Valley, CA).
www.createspace.com

This book may be purchased in bulk for educational, business, or promotional use. For information, please e-mail peterkgreer@gmail.com.

Cover design by HanroogMOU.
99designs.com/users/1428777

Cover photos by Nikole Lim.
freelyinhope.org

Author photo by Jeremy Cowart.
jeremycowart.com

Keith and Peter Greer

Dedicated to Mr. Resh at Landisville Primary School

Watching Seeds Grow

A Guide to Entrepreneurship for Parents and Children

Keith Greer and Peter Greer

Foreword by Chloe Smiley

CONTENTS

FOREWORD

In second grade, I decided to start my own nonprofit. Combining two of my passions, sewing rudimentary sachets and helping a local homeless shelter, I recruited five playmates and started a small "factory" in a spare Sunday School classroom. With little fingers furiously turning out potpourri-filled sachets, we then sold our product to the congregation and donated the profits to the homeless shelter.

It's been 13 years and countless in-house businesses since my first entrepreneurial pursuits. While my business interests have widely varied, from creating candles to custom greeting cards to healthcare apps, I have never lost my love of creating unique solutions to the problems surrounding me. I am continually inspired by the innovation of others, especially in youth who are usually relegated to babysitting and fast food jobs.

The support of my family in my entrepreneurship has been invaluable, even if it was just my mom telling my sister that it was fair if I wanted to charge a quarter for her to play my latest game. My parents instilled in me a belief that I could do anything I put my mind to and that my age was an advantage, not a barrier, to starting my own businesses.

This book combines two incredibly powerful forces to cultivate the entrepreneurial spirit in youth: compelling narrative and practical equipping.

My parents did not simply provide emotional support for my entrepreneurial endeavors; rather, they set me up for success by teaching me financial literacy. From the time I turned five, my parents made sure I understood budgeting and how to "act your wage": Every two weeks, I received my allowance in a lump sum and was responsible for dividing the money into old peanut butter jars labeled short-term savings, long-term savings, tithe, spending money, and taxes. The gift of teaching your children how to spend, save, and give is one that will equip them for life-long success.

The story of Keith Greer starting his own bean-selling business in Rwanda and the other tales of youth entrepreneurship recounted in this book prove that it is possible to be an entrepreneur at any age and in any context. These kids were successful not because they were born in Silicon Valley but simply because they had an idea and took steps to make it a reality. That is the drive and creativity that our families, communities, and country need to thrive. As a parent, you have an exciting role to play in encouraging that innovative spirit.

The Greers' story will help parents unleash their young entrepreneurs and help emerging entrepreneurs pursue their dreams. As you begin this adventure of exploring entrepreneurship with your children, I would like to leave you with my dad's advice that has driven me to continually seek creative solutions: "Nothing is impossible. Impossible just takes a little longer."

Chloe Smiley
Entrepreneur, Co-Founder of Kin Threads and
HealthQuest

INTRODUCTION

After playing in our backyard, we recently asked a group of neighborhood children two questions:

Question #1: Where does our food come from?

Their responses included Giant, Weis, the local market, and a host of other grocery stores.

Even though we live in Lancaster, Pennsylvania, no one answered "a farm."

Question #2: Where do our clothes come from?

Similar to the first question, their responses included the retail outlets where we shop. Target. The Gap. Walmart. The mall.[1]

In both questions, their answers missed any connection to the people who actually made the clothes or grew the food.

Is it possible we are slowly forgetting where our food, clothes, and almost everything else we enjoy originates? We only see the ending point and neglect to remember each of these items has an origin. *When we lose sight of the source of production, the human element is also lost.* In each case, the starting point for items we enjoy is a story of an entrepreneur.

As we distance ourselves from simple stories of creating and producing, entrepreneurship in the United States will continue to experience a steady decline. Today,

---

[1] Thanks to Matt Buckwalter for the idea of asking these questions.

more businesses are closing than being created, a trend that isn't positive for our communities or our families.[2]

Without entrepreneurship, we lose the ability to create *new* stories and discover *new* solutions. From inventing alternative ways to distribute food to rewiring the way we communicate, entrepreneurs enable us to solve problems.

We need the stories of entrepreneurs, for it is through entrepreneurship that we are able to use our gifts, creativity, and skills to create value in our community. Healthy businesses are essential in a flourishing society.

Our hope is that this book may help unlock our imagination to the power of creating and growing. Seeing simple stories of entrepreneurship, perhaps our children will begin to discover the joy of seeing needs and creating innovative solutions. In some small way, perhaps we could plant seeds of creativity and watch these entrepreneurial seeds grow in the next generation.

The first part of this book tells the story of how Keith's eyes were opened to stories of entrepreneurship while on a trip to Rwanda. Section two equips parents with 10 steps to unleash your young entrepreneur.

We hope these stories entertain and encourage you to begin your own entrepreneurial adventures. Please share your stories with us at www.watchingseedsgrow.com.

Keep growing,
Keith and Peter

---

[2] See more at The Institute for Faith and Work's blog, http://blog.tifwe.org/the-entrepreneurial-generation/.

SECTION 1

THREE BAGS OF BEANS

For Kids: Stories of Youth Entrepreneurship from Around the World

CHAPTER ONE: KEITH'S BEANS

"Hey Dad, can I go play outside?"

Little did I know, this simple question would begin an unexpected adventure.

My dad and I had been in Rwanda for a week, a country in East Africa, learning about *microfinance*, a big word that simply means helping men and women start businesses so they can provide for their families.

We visited markets, which are like shopping malls in the United States, with many people buying and selling things right next to each other. But unlike a mall, in markets men and women sit at booths outdoors instead of indoors. We met a woman who sewed clothes and school uniforms, a man who cut hair in an outdoor barbershop, and a family who raised chickens.

With only a couple more days in Rwanda, my dad was in a meeting indoors. Seeing the sun shining outdoors, I was ready to get out and explore. After convincing my dad I wouldn't get into any trouble, my dad replied, "Sure, Keith. Just stay close."

Walking outside the brick building with a tin roof, I hiked down a dirt path and saw a field. As I got closer, I saw it had recently been harvested. Its crop: beans. Leaning over and looking closer, I discovered there were still a few remaining bean pods. Picking one up and opening it, I saw bright red and white beans, just like the ones I had eaten the night before.

Off to the right was another bean. Up a little farther, I saw a couple more.

Discovering a small discarded bag, I started filling it with these forgotten beans. Over the next few minutes, I had filled three small bags.

Walking back to the brick building, I proudly showed my dad what I had discovered.

My dad exclaimed, "What beautiful beans! But are you sure you are allowed to take them?"

Just to be sure, we checked with the gardener and learned that these truly were discarded beans, and we were free to take them with us (and next time, I promised my dad I will ask first!).

I had planned to bring these beans home. But then I remembered the men and women we had met selling in the market.

If they could have a business, perhaps I could too.

Returning to Kigali, the capital city of Rwanda, I asked my dad about the idea.

"Would you take me to the market so I can sell my beans?"

Dad replied, "Keith, it's impossible to sell these beans in the market."

I wasn't so sure, so I asked, "But why? I know I can sell these beans!"

After a few more minutes of conversation, my dad agreed.

"Okay, let's give it a try."

So we went to find the outdoor market. Walking through several streets, we saw a shop selling fruits and vegetables. I approached a man standing behind a giant bag of beans.

"Would you like to buy my beans?" I asked.

To ensure I was communicating clearly, I held up my three bags of beans.

The shopkeeper replied, "No thank you, I already have all the beans I need."

My dad asked me, "Want to go back home?"

I responded, "Not yet. We need to keep trying!"

Walking for 10 more minutes, we came to another shop owner with a bright shirt and an even brighter smile. I asked my question again.

"Want to buy my beans?"

His grin widened, probably surprised to see an eight-year-old American boy in a Rwandan market selling beans.

The shopkeeper asked, "How much?"

I answered, "20 Rwandan francs."

With an even BIGGER smile, he said, "Yego" (which means "yes") and purchased all three bags of my beans.

With the money I had just earned, I thought about buying a toy. But instead, I decided to buy more beans so I could see if other shopkeepers were interested in buying small bags of beans.

I learned this is called *reinvesting*.

Over the next three days, I bought and sold more beans, developing friendships with many people in the market. I learned some people didn't want to buy large amounts of beans, and preferred my small bags at a good price. They also enjoyed that I would bring the beans right to them, being as convenient as possible.

I discovered it was possible to turn time into money and have a lot of fun in the process!

Interacting with the shopkeepers, I heard their stories of how they started their businesses. Each business owner was able to answer the following seven questions:

Plan. What are you going to do?

Product. What are you going to create?

Price. How much will it cost?

Packaging. What will make it stand out?

Place. Where will you sell?

Promotion. How will you gain attention?

Profit. When you look at all your costs, are you earning more than you are spending?

As I kept selling beans, I discovered my own answers to these questions, and kept improving how I packaged them and sold them.

After several more trips to the market buying and selling beans, I had earned 3,500 francs (about $7), which is a lot of money considering I had started with nothing other than three small bags of beans!

I learned that this was called *profit*. Profit is the money that is left over when you take how much money you made from selling something and subtract how much it cost for you to sell your product.

The last evening in Rwanda, after selling my last bag of beans, I took one final trip to the market to buy a pineapple. I was going to miss my friends in the market who had taught me so much about the basics of starting a business.

After dinner, we enjoyed the pineapple with Maggie and Jean Louis, who were our hosts in Rwanda. With juice dripping down my chin, I realized that starting a business can taste delicious.

> **Keith Tip:**
> **Nobody expects kids to be entrepreneurs. Use that to your advantage, and you'll quickly earn your first customers.**

CHAPTER TWO: MUCO'S DONUTS

Back in Lancaster, Pennsylvania, I couldn't wait to tell my friends about Rwanda, the people we met, how microfinance was helping people, and my bean business.

My good friend Muco was one of the people most excited to hear my stories. Muco was born in Rwanda but now lives in the United States. After describing my bean business, Muco explained how he had recently started his own small business in Lancaster.

"How cool! I went from the U.S. to Rwanda and started a small business, and you came from Rwanda to the U.S. to start your small business," I said.

Sitting down with Muco, I asked him to tell me his story.

Muco explained, "A few weeks ago, I brought beignets, a type of African donut, to my English class— and they were a big hit. As soon as they were gone, my friends asked if they could buy some more. My response was, 'Sure!'"

I asked, "What did you do next?"

Muco kept telling me his story, "Over the next week, I took orders from friends. And it wasn't just my friends from English class. People all throughout the school heard about my donuts."

Now I was really curious! I asked Muco, "What price did you sell them for?"

Muco said, "I decided to sell them for $1 per donut, but if someone bought 10 or more, I discounted the price to 50 cents. Many people ordered in bulk, and three people bought 20!"

"How did you make the donuts?" I wondered.

Muco answered, "Because people paid me when they placed their order, I had the money to go to the local grocery store and purchase flour, sugar, oil, spices, and the other ingredients. Returning home, I mixed the ingredients together in a bowl. Then I dropped small lumps of dough into boiling oil on the stove. I had my mom's help with this part, since you have to be very careful the oil doesn't splash on you. That hurts."

I told Muco, "I highly recommend you do this again! In fact, can I buy some donuts from you? I had these donuts in Rwanda, and they are delicious."

> **Keith Tip:**
> *Sell what you know. Muco was the perfect person to start a beignet business because he and his family knew how to make them. What makes you and your family special?*

Thinking through Muco's business, I realized he had answered the same seven questions:

Plan. What are you going to do?

His plan was to sell African donuts to his classmates.

Product. What are you going to sell?

Beignets, a type of African donut.

Price. How much will it cost?

$1 per donut, or 50 cents per donut for bulk purchases.

Packaging. What will make it stand out?

He placed each donut in a bag with a napkin.

Place. Where will you sell?

To his friends at school.

Promotion. How will you gain attention?

Word of mouth (speaking to people), and by giving away samples to his English class.

Profit.   When you look at all your costs, are you earning more than you are spending?

Definitely. Because customers preordered the donuts, Muco knew exactly how many ingredients he needed. After adding up how much it would cost to make the donuts, Muco figured out how much to charge for them by adding a *mark-up*, or the amount of profit he wanted to make on each donut. That way, he could make sure that he would make more money on the donuts than he was spending to make them!

Inspired by Muco's story, I began to see entrepreneurs all around me, including an unexpected visit to my friend's church.

CHAPTER THREE: SAVANNAH AND MIA'S BEAN CANDLES

Early on a Sunday morning, I got in the car with my dad and drove to Willowdale Chapel. We were told they were having a "Congo Christmas Market" where many kids had started their own businesses.

As a way of raising funds for HOPE International, where my dad works, each person created something to sell. The money raised that day went to help men and women start small businesses in the Democratic Republic of Congo.

Walking through the lobby, we saw handmade jewelry. Crosses made from nails. Christmas ornaments. Hand woven hats. But given my interest in beans, I was immediately intrigued by what the Jeffery family created.

Approaching their family's table, I met Savannah and Mia. They had created bean candles.

I asked them, "Where did you get the idea to make bean candles?"

Mia answered, "Our grandmother taught us! She showed us how to use different colored beans, like lentils. After we put the beans in a jar, we placed a candle in the middle. That's how we made our bean candles."

Savannah and Mia quickly realized that these candles could not only be used in their home but that they could sell them too. They used their allowances to buy more beans, jars, and candles to make enough candles to sell at the Market.

Just like Muco, Savannah and Mia had to think through the 7 P's in order to make and sell their bean candles.

Plan.   What are you going to do?

Savannah and Mia planned to make bean candles to sell at the Market to raise funds for HOPE International.

Product.   What are you going to sell?

Candles in candleholders made from a jar and beans. They also knit hats to sell.

Price.   How much will it cost?

$5 for a candle (we bought two!).

Packaging.   What will make it stand out?

The different colored beans made the candles unique.

Place.   Where will you sell?

The sisters sold their candles and hats at the Market at their church.

Promotion.   How will you gain attention?

The entire church knew about the Market and the members were excited to see what each child created.

Profit.　　　　When you look at all your costs, are you earning more than you are spending?

Yes. Savannah and Mia made more money than it cost to make the candles and hats so that they could donate the extra money to HOPE International.

They were using their creativity to create a product and give the proceeds to help others start businesses all around the world.

And they were doing it through bean candles.

> *Keith Tip:*
> *Giving is an important part of having a business. Savannah and Mia had a lot of fun selling their products and knowing they were helping a great cause.*

CHAPTER FOUR: OWEN AND WILL'S BUDDY BARS

After beginning to realize what kid entrepreneurs were doing, my dad and I started searching for even more examples—and we were amazed at what we found.

We found a really creative family in Austin, Texas, the Shafers, who created Buddy Bars. We asked if we could interview them, and they were willing to tell us another amazing story of youth entrepreneurship.

For several years, this was a family interested in learning about the businesses all around them. As a family, they visited local businesses to hear their stories, like a pizza place, a taco store, and an energy bar company.

After visiting the local taco store, the owner gave them 50 tacos for them to start selling. The Shafer family loaded up the tacos onto their wagon and took them around the neighborhood.

Remember the P that stood for Promotion? Well, the Shafer kids found out how important that P is when they sold their tacos. They hung up flyers telling their neighbors about the tacos the night before they took their wagon around their neighborhood and had lots of people wanting to buy their tacos!

Later, knowing their interest in entrepreneurship, their babysitter told them about a local business fair and encouraged them to join.

The business fair was for kids just like me. Over one hundred kids each rented an area to sell their products or services. After seeing how much fun it was to sell tacos and make some money from working hard, the Shafer kids wanted to be a part of it.

Malia, the youngest in the Shafer family, wasn't old enough to sign up so she helped at home. Her older brother, Owen, and his buddy, Will, decided to go into business together. Owen told us that he and Will had been buddies since birth and they discovered that business ideas are often most enjoyable when they're done together.

Once they decided to be part of the business fair, they sat down and thought, "What business should we do?" This was like when Muco decided to make donuts—they were making a plan, the first P of starting a business.

I asked Owen, "How did you come up with your idea of what to make and sell?"

"We needed to get energy because we love to play and stuff. So Buddy Bars was born!" Owen explained.

This is how many businesses are started. Someone sees a need. Owen and Will realized they got hungry while they were out playing. And they came up with a solution: an energy bar that other people would also want to eat!

Owen and Will had their business idea, but there was still a lot of work to do before the business fair. They had to decide what kind of bars they wanted to make, find the recipes, test the bars, and package them!

"How did you decide which flavor bars to make?" I asked.

Owen answered, "We just created bars based on the kinds of foods we like to eat, like chocolate, cherries, and peanut butter. It is a lot more fun to work on a business if you are selling something you really like!"

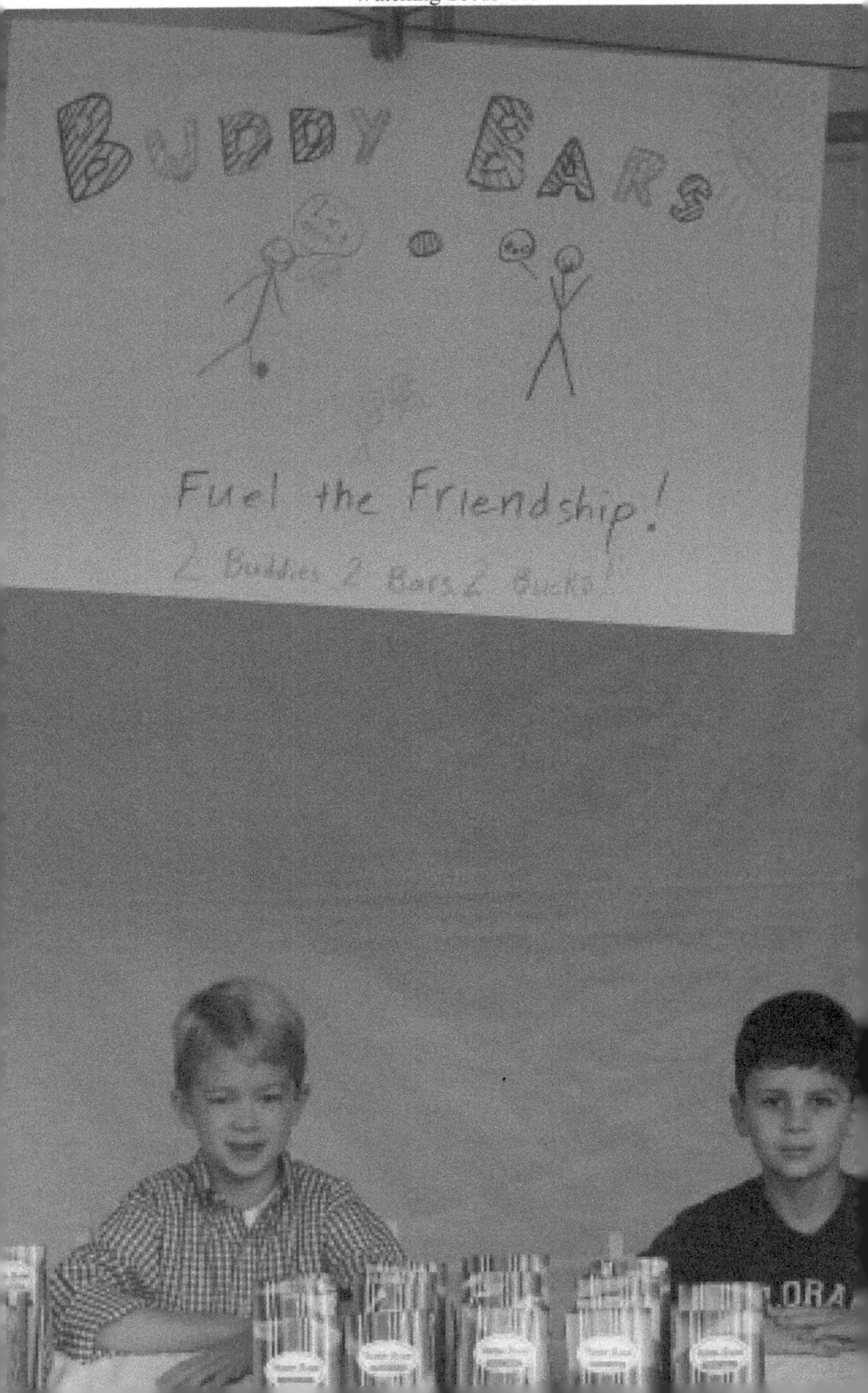
Buddy Bars
Fuel the Friendship!
2 Buddies 2 Bars 2 Bucks!

I was realizing how important it was to believe in your business and work with people that you can trust and that believe in the business too!

Owen and Will had so much fun making and selling the bars that they decided to keep Buddy Bars going after the business fair. Owen's dad helped them get set up at a farmers' market nearby, where lots of people come to sell fruit, vegetables, or other food they made. Owen and Will learned at the business fair that their bars started to melt when they were in the sun, so they changed the recipe before selling the energy bars outside at the farmers' market.

> *Keith Tip:*
> *Being an entrepreneur means that you have to always be ready to change your product to make sure it is something people would really want to buy and use. Or in the case of Buddy Bars, eat!*

I was definitely beginning to see a pattern. All of the kids that started a business had spent a lot of time thinking about how they were going to start and keep their business going. Owen and Will used the same 7 P's that Muco, Savannah, Mia, and I had!

Plan. What are you going to do?

Owen and Will were going to have a booth at the business fair and sell Buddy Bars.

Product. What are you going to sell?

Buddy Bars—homemade energy bars in three flavors: Rockin' Chocolate, Chillin' Cherry, and Partyin' Peanut Butter.

Price.   How much will it cost?

$2 for each bar.

Packaging.   What will make it stand out?

Owen and Will wrapped the bars in colorful papers and put a sticker on them with their logo.

Place.   Where will you sell?

They sold Buddy Bars at the Children's Business Fair and then at the East Austin Farmers' Market.

Promotion.   How will you gain attention?

Owen and Will made a sign with their business's name to hang up at the business fair. They also came up with the phrase, "Fuel the Friendship," so that people would remember their business. They also made a page on Facebook about Buddy Bars.

Profit.   When you look at all your costs, are you earning more than you are spending?

Yes! Owen and Will were really excited to spend their extra money at the business fair on products that other kids were selling. They also put the money that they made from selling Buddy Bars into making more bars.

My eyes were opened to stories of entrepreneurship all around me. Kids' creativity is everywhere—and a lot of times, it tastes delicious.

But the best part is that all of our stories are just beginning.

SECTION 2

WATCHING SEEDS GROW

For Parents: 10 Steps to Unleash Your Young Entrepreneur

"Hey Dad, can I go play outside?"

When my son asked me that question, I had no idea it was going to start a family journey to learn about entrepreneurship. The stories Keith told in the first pages of this book are powerful in their simplicity, as his eyes were opened to examples of entrepreneurship all around us. We have no idea how these ideas will shape his life. However, with absolute certainty, the journey itself has brought us closer together and been exceptionally positive in building self-esteem and creating shared memories.

Paul Shafer, father of the Shafer kids who shared their story about Buddy Bars in the first half of the book, has been a self-proclaimed "wanna-preneur" his entire life. He intentionally chose to instill the concepts and excitement for entrepreneurship in his family, so that they learn hard work, innovation, perseverance, and creativity. He believes that "the values associated with entrepreneurism are good life skills. Entrepreneurism is the vehicle for learning real world values."[1]

Seeing the positive benefits of exploring entrepreneurship, our hope is that this book equips you to start your own journey with your family and friends.

Designed to be as practical as possible, this book walks you through 10 steps of entrepreneurial development for you and your child.

We would love to hear your stories! Tell us about your family's entrepreneurial adventures at www.watchingseedsgrow.com.

---

[1] Interview with Paul Shafer, June 19, 2014.

STEP 1: START WITH STORIES

Kids tire quickly of lectures, but stories entertain and engage. Thankfully, stories of entrepreneurship are all around us.

To cast a vision of entrepreneurship for your kids, tell them your simple stories. Most of us weren't child dot.com prodigies, but we all have a story about our first lemonade stand, lawn mowing businesses, and how we ended up where we are now. If you're not an entrepreneur, maybe those in your family have been. Did a great-grandfather start a restaurant? Does an aunt have her own beauty salon?

Instead of "business" being a vague and confusing topic, it becomes Aunt Judy's sporting goods store or your childhood adventures trying to sell painted rocks as doorstoppers to the neighbors. Suddenly, becoming an entrepreneur is an achievable and exciting goal for your kids.

Beyond your personal stories, you are surrounded by entrepreneurs. It could be the owner of a local restaurant franchise, the CEO of a major corporation, or a family-owned grocery store. Invite them to come and talk at your kids' school, churches, or clubs. If they directly produce a product, having samples are a great way to grab kids' attention and give them something tangible to associate with entrepreneurship. Hearing stories of entrepreneurship helps kids to start thinking about how they can create something of their own.

Fred Rogers (known as Mister Rogers), the beloved icon of children's television known for his sweaters and

warm personality, understood the power of showing examples of entrepreneurship. As a regular part of *Mister Rogers' Neighborhood*, which aired more than 30 years, Mister Rogers went to a business and showed how a product was made—like crayons or graham crackers.

Following Mister Rogers' example, consider fostering an interest in entrepreneurship by visiting a local business. While there may not be a Crayola factory down the street from you, most local businesses are open and excited to give a tour of their operations and explain why they do what they do. Start with your kids' favorite restaurant, toy store, or ice cream shop. They will not only learn that products do not just mysteriously appear on shelves—but that working to create them can be great fun and create value.

With just a little looking, it is possible to celebrate stories of entrepreneurship all around you. The Shafer family found this to be a valuable experience for them. While listening to stories of other entrepreneurs, they began realizing the potential to start a business comes in many avenues. In fact, seeds were planted for Owen and Will to start Buddy Bars—their own energy bar business—after they went to visit a local energy bar company. You can find out more about how the Shafer parents cast an entrepreneurial vision for their children on their blog: shaferpower.com.

Another practical way to explore entrepreneurship with your children is through online resources that link kids with others modeling entrepreneurship. One such website is actonhero.org. Here, you and your kids can explore the stories of a variety of different kinds of entrepreneurs. Many of these self-starters began when they were young and have valuable lessons to share about their trailblazing into the business world.

When learning about other young entrepreneurs, Keith saw a pattern of P's. These 7 P's provide the building blocks of a successful business. In the Appendix, you will find a Business Plan Worksheet and a Business Plan Template. While visiting businesses, encourage children to use the Business Plan Worksheet to identify the 7 P's (Plan, Product, Price, Packaging, Place, Promotion, and Profit). Identifying these simple steps in other businesses will be helpful when children begin to explore starting their own.

The Business Plan Worksheet is a place to help kids start brainstorming different elements of a business. Once they fill it out, they are ready to explore the details of their business plan. Each section of the Business Plan Worksheet correlates with a section on the Business Plan Template, which allows kids to present their business in a clean and professional way. Both are located at the back of this book in Appendix 2.

Once kids are excited about entrepreneurship and starting their own businesses, you can use this adventure as a valuable learning opportunity to build a foundation of financial literacy. The next few steps will guide you through that educational process.

STEP 2: START A SAVINGS ACCOUNT

According to the paper titled "Financial Literacy—Does it Matter?" by Lewis Mandell, an economics and finance professor, a consumer that is "thrifty or savings-oriented is less likely to experience financial failure than one who is not thrifty or is consumption-oriented."[2]

However, trends show us that Americans are no longer saving like they used to. According to Milton Marquis in the Federal Reserve Bank of San Francisco's *Economic Letters*:

"From 1980 through 1994, the U.S. saving rate averaged 8%; thereafter, it fell steeply, and since mid-2000... it has averaged approximately 1%."[3]

This is troubling for obvious reasons. Without savings, families are more vulnerable to financial failure caused by rather commonplace life events like losing a job, a family member growing ill, or needing to replace a car or other expensive asset.[4]

As many parents know, if we do not start good habits early, they are much harder to form later. If we do not save and give when we earn $1, then there is no reason to think that we will give or save when we earn $50,000. It is never too early to start teaching your kids to be responsible with whatever money they have.

---

[2] Lewis Mandell, "Financial Literacy: Does it Matter?" Jump$tart Coalition for Personal Financial Literacy, April 8, 2005, http://jumpstart.org/clearinghouse7.html, 2.

[3] Milton Marquis, "What's Behind the Low U.S. Personal Saving Rate?" *FRBSF Economic Letters*, March 29, 2002, http://www.frbsf.org/economic-research/publications/economic-letter/2002/march/what-is-behind-the-low-us-personal-saving-rate/.

[4] Ibid.

Most banks offer a child's savings account. When the monthly statement comes, you can have your kids understand their balance. If it is an interest-bearing account, they can keep track of what their money is earning using the Savings Account Worksheet (Appendix 3).

Alternatively, you can always use the "3 Jar Allowance System" created by Larry Burkett[5] and also promoted by Dave Ramsey. [6] Give your kids three to five peanut butter jars and let them decorate the jars as they wish. Label one of the jars for short-term savings (purchases you want to make in a year), long-term savings (a car, college, etc.), spending money, and tithing money. Or make up your own categories! What categories do you think would help teach your children how to save?

---

[5]Larry Burkett, "Teaching kids with a pre-budget," 100.7 Christian Talk, http://www.kgftradio.com/507246/print/.

[6]Dave Ramsey, "The Art of Raising a Money Superstar," daveramsey.com, February 24, 2012, http://www.daveramsey.com/article/the-art-of-raising-a-money-superstar/lifeandmoney_kidsandmoney/.

STEP 3: TEACH FINANCIAL LITERACY

More and more of today's students have been proven to be financially illiterate. When students were first surveyed by Jump$tart Coalition based in Washington, D.C., in 1998, the average score students received on financial literacy was 57 percent—the equivalent of a D+. Since then Jump$tart has surveyed students every two years, and recently, students received an F; they got 50 percent of the 31 financial literacy questions wrong.[7]

The multiple choice questions in the survey cover a variety of financial literacy questions like revenue, taxes, savings, and investment. For example, here is one of the questions used in the 2008 survey:

Question 5. Under which of the following circumstances would it be financially beneficial to you to borrow money to buy something now and repay it with future income?

a) When you need to buy a car to get a much better paying job.

b) When you really need a week vacation.

c) When some clothes you like go on sale.

d) When the interest on the loan is greater than the interest you get on your savings.[8]

This should not be a question we want our children to get wrong, and yet basic questions of finances and budgeting are consistently missed by too many.

---

[7] Lewis Mandell, "Financial Literacy: Does it Matter?" Jump Start Coalition for Personal Financial Literacy, April 8, 2005,
http://jumpstart.org/clearinghouse7.html, 2.

[8] Lewis Mandell, "The Financial Literacy of Young American Adults: Results of the 2008 National Jump$tart Coalition Survey of High School Seniors and College Students," Washington D.C.: The Jump$tart Coalition for Personal Financial Literacy, 2009, 167.

No one wants their child to graduate high school making the wrong financial decisions half the time. Entrepreneurial activities have the potential to ensure that your children are above the national average on financial literacy by the time they are in middle school.

Even if your kids never start a business on their own, they will always be dealing with money. Learning entrepreneurship at a young age teaches kids the value of a dollar, a proper perspective on money, and how important it is to save.

Numerous resources are available online to help teach your children financial literacy.

- PNC has partnered with Sesame Street to create a web program called "'S' is for Savings."
  - https://www1.pnc.com/sisforsavings/
- If you don't want to use real money, other virtual tools like bankingkids.com allow children to become familiar with financial terms and forms.
  - http://www.bankingkids.com/pages/ed_1.html
- Wells Fargo has created a financial literacy curriculum called "Hands-on-Banking" that is a fun and comprehensive resource for teaching your children financial literacy. The section on Savings and Checking (Page 35) is especially helpful.
  - http://www.handsonbanking.org/en/resources/Kids_T_Guide.pdf
- Crown Ministries also provides workbooks to help teach children about financial wisdom.
  - http://store.crown.org/category_s/168.html
- The Young Americans Bank is a one-of-a-kind bank specifically designed for young people ages 21 and younger.

- o http://yacenter.org/young-americans-bank/
- Junior Achievement is geared toward teachers but can be a valuable resource for parents as well.
  - o https://www.juniorachievement.org/web/ja-usa/home

This next section focuses on developing the character traits necessary for entrepreneurial success. The world does not just need more entrepreneurs, but rather needs entrepreneurs with integrity, character, a strong work ethic, and generosity.

STEP 4: TEACH THE PRINCIPLE OF HARD WORK

The American Institute of CPAs surveyed the amount of money that parents give their kids for allowance. In the U.S., the average allowance a child receives in a year could purchase an Apple iPad and three Kindles, and the child still could have pocket change left over. Since only 1 percent of parents said their kids save any part of their allowance, almost all that money is being spent each year.

The financial literacy test done by the Jump$tart Coalition found that children who received a regular allowance—and were not required to do chores to earn their allowance—were the least financially literate and least thrifty of any student group surveyed.[9]

With an unearned allowance, kids quickly learn that money *really* does grow on trees—or in this case, out of mom and dad's wallet. An entitled attitude can be the result of such unearned success. And this entitled attitude will not only hinder children's ability to budget effectively but also infect other areas of their lives and harm how they problem-solve.

Many families are moving beyond a "no-strings attached" allowance and requiring household chores to earn their allowance. This becomes an opportunity to teach your children the relationship between effort and

---

[9] Lewis Mandell, "Financial Literacy: Does it Matter?" Jump Start Coalition for Personal Financial Literacy, April 8, 2005, http://jumpstart.org/clearinghouse7.html, 10.

reward. If no jobs are done, then quite simply, there is no allowance.

In our home, we have chores we ask the kids to do every day, such as bringing down the laundry, making their beds, and sweeping the floor. Beyond the core jobs, we also allow our children to do "above-and-beyond" chores where they can earn additional funds. In our laundry room, we place a magnet over the names of the above-and-beyond chores listed, along with the dollar bills showing how much they will earn. This gives your kids a chance to make some extra spending money they would not have otherwise and gets some household jobs done in the meantime!

Eventually, as kids get older, they will desire more money than their allowance allows. This is the perfect time to encourage kids to start businesses outside of the house and reach customers beyond family members.

STEP 5: TEACH THE PRINCIPLE OF PERSONAL OWNERSHIP

Growing up, we would visit my grandparents in Lancaster, Pennsylvania. Part of the visit would always include a trip to Kitchen Kettle village, where we would taste endless samples and watch Amish families make jams and jellies.

We often would venture into a small shop stocked to overflowing with antiques. Besides the bizarre porcelain clowns, the most terrifying part of this experience were the signs posted everywhere warning us, "If you break it, you buy it," always accompanied with a clip art sad face. In a room jam-packed with ancient glass figurines, we figured it was hopeless to make it out unscathed.

We have all seen these menacing signs, warning careless shoppers that they will be responsible for paying for any damaged merchandise. As condescending or scary as they may seem, these signs represent an important life concept.

Personal ownership is an antidote to entitlement. If kids receive a legitimate way to earn their money, they will start developing intrinsic motivation because they understand ownership.[10] Suddenly, this is not just some toy their parents gave them that can be easily replaced; it is a treasured belonging that they sacrificed their own hard-earned money to purchase. You will experience relief

---

[10] Richard and Linda Eyre, *The Entitlement Trap: How to Rescue Your Child with a New Family System of Choosing, Earning, and Ownership*, New York, New York: Penguin Group (USA) Inc., 2011, 75.

when the doe-eyed begging for money stops. And you'll be wide-eyed in wonder at how much better kids treat their belongings when they personally invest in them. Encouraging kids to take more personal ownership also means resisting the urge to automatically fix the problems that come up and instead let them pay for their mistakes—in business or otherwise!

In *The Entitlement Trap*, authors Richard and Linda Eyre share how ownership creates a positive ripple effect of character development: "If the *perception* of ownership can be given to children, a sense of responsibility will follow, and a sense of pride, and a sense of purpose."[11]

While I would not suggest printing, "You break it, you buy it" warning signs and posting them around your house, the principle of personal accountability teaches children financial responsibility. If their actions have no consequences, you miss an opportunity to shape your children's character.

---

[11] Richard and Linda Eyre, *The Entitlement Trap: How to Rescue Your Child with a New Family System of Choosing, Earning, and Ownership*, New York, New York: Penguin Group (USA) Inc., 2011, 33.

STEP 6: TEACH THE PRINCIPLE OF INVESTMENT

Another practical way to encourage entrepreneurial creativity in your kids is to give them the $10 challenge.

When Pastor Brian Smilde challenged his congregation, Immanuel Reformed Church in Grand Rapids, Michigan, to give away $10 after a sermon on giving, he had no idea that his $10 would multiply 1,000 times over. (Read more of his story in the link referenced in footnotes.)[12]

When we heard this story at HOPE International, we decided to try it for ourselves. Instead of just asking our friends to give away $10, we asked them to see how much money they could make with the sum after two weeks. Though a simple exercise, this game is a powerful example of the benefits of investment and being creative in making money.

Below is how to play:

- Challenge your kids and their friends to turn $10 into as much money as they can in two weeks.
- Whoever makes the most money at the end of the two weeks wins!
- Give them basic parameters:
- You must buy all the supplies for your venture like lemonade ingredients or car-wash equipment.

---

[12] Jan Holst, "Local church's $10 challenge results in $11,000 in gifts and is still growing," mLive, January 12, 2012, http://www.mlive.com/east-grand-rapids/index.ssf/2012/01/post_38.html.

- You can only use $10 to make business-related purchases, but spend as much time as you'd like to invest in your business within those two weeks.

- Get creative and have fun!

- Money is never free. At the end of two weeks, they will have to return the $10, as well as an extra $1 to pay for the opportunity to use $10 for those two weeks. Explain how this $1 is the interest and that paying $1 to use $10 is a 10 percent interest rate.

- Any money that you make after paying back the $11 ($10 loan + $1 interest) is yours to give away or spend.

- To kick off the challenge, have them create a poster board to keep track of how much money they are making so that they can see how their other siblings or friends are doing.

- Give them worksheets (Appendix 4) for keeping track of costs, sales, and profit.

If they really latch onto this new adventure of running a business and making their own money, encourage your kids to keep the business running past the two-week mark. The Business Plan Worksheet (Appendix 2) at the back of the book is a helpful tool for kids who want to take their business idea to the next level.

STEP 7: TEACH THE PRINCIPLE OF GENEROSITY

Keith turned his three small bags of beans into 3,500 francs in three days. As proud as I was of his entrepreneurial spirit and initiative, what he did with the money brought me even more joy. On his own, Keith used a significant portion of his earnings to buy a pineapple to share with our host family.

It is important to teach kids the satisfaction that comes from giving. The best way to teach your children the principle of generosity is to model a giving spirit yourself. Rachel Ramsey—daughter of financial advisor, author, and radio host Dave Ramsey—cited the joy of giving as one of the most important financial lessons her parents taught her at a young age.[13]

Whether your kids are getting their money from their own business or an earned allowance, encourage them to make a category for giving. In addition to training children about handling money responsibly from a young age, teaching them that giving away a portion of what they earn is a part of doing business will help our kids create healthy habits of saving and giving for the rest of their lives. One simple way to do that is to encourage your kids to tithe 10 percent of their profits to their church or Sunday School or favorite organization.

The "aha!" moment for kids often occurs when they see tangible results of giving. The reality, though, is most kids will not make enough income to give a donation large enough for visible results. One way to see more of the

---

[13] "Money Lessons Kids Aren't Taught in School," daveramsey.com, September 28, 2011, http://www.daveramsey.com/article/money-lessons-kids-arent-taught-in-school/lifeandmoney_kidsandmoney/kidstext2/.

results of giving is to work together as a family to help a specific organization or cause.

You can let your little entrepreneurs unleash their creativity on this one, all the way from finding unique ways to use their money to helping others to create a poster board to track their progress.

Rachel Ramsey recalls her own experience with family giving: "Looking back now, it's obvious to me that my $13 didn't buy the tractor trailer full of bikes my family took to inner-city kids," Rachel said. "But as a 10-year-old, there was a connection there when we were out delivering those bikes and seeing those kids' faces light up. I got to know I helped with that."[14]

---

[14] "Money Lessons Kids Aren't Taught in School," daveramsey.com, September 28, 2011, http://www.daveramsey.com/article/money-lessons-kids-arent-taught-in-school/lifeandmoney_kidsandmoney/kidstext2/.

STEP 8: CREATE THE PLAN

While some kids seem like they are born with ideas on how to start a business, others will need a bit more encouragement. It is important that they personally own any projects, but you can play a crucial role in helping them brainstorm and pointing them in the right direction.

Ask your children what makes them most excited and what activities they enjoy the most. These make great springboards. Once they have identified an area that they would like to pursue further (this could be a favorite sport, baking, crafts, electronics, animals, etc.), encourage your kids to niches where they could do something better or fix a problem. Here are two simple questions that have consistently led to surprisingly creative and effective businesses.

- What bothered you today?
- What could you do to make it better?

Just remind your kids that "my sibling" and "sending them away to boarding school" are not acceptable answers to those two questions!

In Appendix 5, you'll find a business brainstorming worksheet that guides kids through the two questions mentioned above as well as some additional prompts to get their creative juices flowing.

STEP 9: LAUNCH AND LEARN

At this point, the financial principles have been taught, the ideas have been brainstormed, and a plan has been created. It is time to launch and learn!

Hockey Hall of Famer Wayne Gretzky famously quipped: "You miss 100 percent of the shots you never take."[15] Many adults have great difficulty in transitioning from the planning to producing stage, so it shouldn't be surprising if your children are hesitant to launch as well. Paul Brown, co-author of *Just Start*, boiled the business starting process down to four simple steps:

1. Act
2. Learn
3. Build
4. Repeat

He adds, "… the key word is to act. You have to act."[16] Have your children use their business plan and start producing and selling! Kids tend to have a built-in customer base. There is nothing wrong with selling to friends and family, especially if they keep in mind their bigger goals to eventually sell to a wider audience.

Steps 2 and 3 of Paul Brown's start-up launch list are also essential. The process of pausing, looking at what is working and what isn't, and then making the necessary changes to fix what's broken is one that many adults

---

[15] Paul B. Brown, "'You miss 100% of the Shots You Don't Take.' You need to Start Shooting at Your Goals," *Forbes*, January 12, 2014, http://www.forbes.com/sites/actiontrumpseverything/2014/01/12/you-miss-100-of-the-shots-you-dont-take-so-start-shooting-at-your-goal/.

[16] Ibid.

struggle to master. However, it is critical to running a business, regardless of your age.

In his book, *Necessary Endings,* Dr. Henry Cloud defines a wise person as one who is open to learning from the experiences life has to offer. Therefore, according to Dr. Cloud, the person who does well is the one who "can learn from his own experience or the experience of others, make that learning a part of himself, and then deliver results from that experience base."[17] Entrepreneurship is an excellent vehicle to teach this valuable lesson to children.

---

[17] Dr. Henry Cloud, *Necessary Endings: The Employees, Businesses, and Relationships that All of Us Have to Give Up in Order to Move Forward,* New York, New York: Harper-Collins Publishers, 2010, 127.

STEP 10: CREATE COMMUNITY

Remember Samantha and Mia? They made hats and bean candles to sell at the "Market" at their church as a fundraiser for HOPE International. They were not the only ones selling things at that market! Dozens of kids participated by making and selling homemade wares.

Whether it is for a cause or just for the pure entrepreneurial fun of it, hosting an Entrepreneurship Fair[18] is a great way to spur on your kids' creativity and create community. This could be done on a small-scale in your neighborhood or through a church, school, or club.

Think of an Entrepreneurship Fair as a kid's version of a farmer's market. Each kid must pay rent for a booth, do their own marketing, bring a unique product to the market, and make a profit! Having numerous booths all vying for customers may be enough competition to get the creativity gears turning, or you could always up the ante and include prizes for Most Creative Advertising, Most Unique Product, etc.

To get ideas or see if there is already a business fair happening in your area, check out these websites:

- Acton Children's Business Fair
  (www.childrensbusinessfair.org)

- TYE young entrepreneurs business plan competitions
  (tye.nathanresearch.com)

---

[18] "About Us," Acton Children's Business Fair, http://www.childrensbusinessfair.org.

- Young Entrepreneur Market
  (www.youngentrepreneurmarket.org/about.html)

There is a full list of Fair rules, advertising ideas, a sample partnership letter, and a sample registration form included in the back of this book as Appendix 6.

FINAL WORD: BE YOUR CHILD'S BIGGEST FAN

After collecting three bags of beans in Rwanda, Keith asked me if we could go and sell them in the market.

Not exactly my shining moment of parental support, my response was, "That's impossible!"

Unintentionally, my response might have shut down his dreaming and cut short his entrepreneurial journey.

I'm very thankful for Keith's persistence as told in the beginning of this book.

As parents, we have the opportunity to be our children's biggest fans—or miss the opportunity to show that we care. Beyond starting a business, this posture of cheering for our kids has a positive impact on a child's entire outlook on life.

Not only is it common sense that being an encouraging presence in our children's lives will positively impact them, but there has also been numerous studies that confirm how encouraging your kids influences them for good. A study done through the Center on Innovation and Improvement at DePaul University found that parents who "hold high expectations for their teens, communicate their expectations clearly, and encourage their adolescents to work hard in order to attain them can make a difference in their students' success."[19]

Starting a business takes courage. This is an opportunity for us to shout louder than the voices of self-

---

[19] Evanthia N. Patrikakou, "The Power of Parent Involvement: Evidence, Ideas, and Tools for Student Success," Center on Innovation and Improvement, 2008, 2.

doubt that highlight challenges and focus on inadequacies. Voices of self-doubt make life's hurdles look seemingly impossible—and such voices ask, *Wouldn't it be easier to simply give up?*

But we want to be the voice cheering our children on.

Regardless of the results, the entrepreneurial journey is an opportunity to let our kids know we are proud of them.

Personally, I'll never forget the times I was on the soccer or lacrosse field and looked over at my parents cheering. My guess is that we never really outgrow the need for our parents' support.

Ask any entrepreneur if it is easy to start a business, and they will probably laugh in response. Starting a new venture takes courage and tenacity. Most entrepreneurs can point to a small number of people who were there for them, supporting them each step of the way.

For our children, let's make sure we are among their most avid supporters and raving fans.

Appendices
Created by Chloe Smiley

Appendix 1: Climbing the Ladder of Success

This book contains 10 steps to help guide you and your child along their entrepreneurial journey. These steps are like rungs on a ladder.

Character must be the foundation for any successful business or life venture. The best entrepreneurs are firmly rooted in a strong work ethic and generous spirit.

Next, **creativity** is essential to creating innovative solutions to the world's needs. Sharing stories is key to unlocking the storehouse of a child's imagination.

Competency is the next rung, enabling the follow-through that a creative entrepreneur with a solid foundation of character needs to turn dreams into reality.

From starting a savings account to hosting an entrepreneurship fair, acquiring and using **capital** wisely is a crucial skill that all entrepreneurs need to keep moving upward and onward.

As parents and mentors, we have a very important role to fill in **cheering** on the young entrepreneurs in our life. This final stage of support and encouragement in entrepreneurial development is key.

CHEERING

CAPITAL

COMPETENCY

CREATIVITY

CHARACTER

Appendix 2: Business Plan Worksheet and Template

PLAN

(1) What is the name of the business?

_____

(2) What is your product or service?

_____

(3) What problem are you solving?

_____

(4) How are you solving that problem?

_____

(5) When did you start your business?

_____

(6) Who are you selling your product or service to?

_____

(7) What do you want to do with your business?

_____

Using the answers to the seven questions from the previous page, fill in your own mission statement!

Mission Statement

(1)_____ is a (2)_____
that helps (3) _____ by (4)
_____. Started on
(5)_____, (1)_____ is
passionate about serving (6) _____ and is
looking to (7) _____.

Mission Statement

_____
_____
_____
_____
_____
_____

PRODUCT

Draw a picture of your product or you performing a
service here!

Picture of product or service

Circle five adjectives that describe your product or service
(or add some of your own!)

innovative	one-of-a-kind	efficient
delicious	quality	sleek
inexpensive		genuine
bold fast	personalized	unique
beautiful daring		colorful sturdy
creative	first	sweet
fresh new		comfortable

Now list the five adjectives that you chose and use them
to write your own product description!

My product is:

_____

_____

_____

_____

_____

Product Description

Here at (Company Name), we provide adjective #1
and adjective #2 (insert product name). We believe
that this (insert product name) is adjective #3 and
adjective #4 and that (what problem does it solve) in
a very adjective #5 way.

Product Description

_____

_____

_____

_____

_____

Growth Stage Questionnaire

1) I have been selling my product or service for:

    a. Less than 4 months

    b. 4-6 months

    c. Around a year

    d. 2 or more years

2) On a typical day, I sell _____ products or services:

    a. Less than 5

    b. 5-19

    c. 20-39

    d. 40+

3) In my town, school, or neighborhood, most people know about my business:

    a. Not true at all

    b. Somewhat true

    c. Definitely true

    d. They used to, but people seem to be forgetting

4) I would say that my business is:

    a. Just starting out

    b. Growing like crazy!

    c. Never been better

    d. Losing steam

Answer Key

Mostly A's: Introduction

Mostly B's: Growth Phase

Mostly C's: Maturity Phase

Mostly D's: Declining Phase

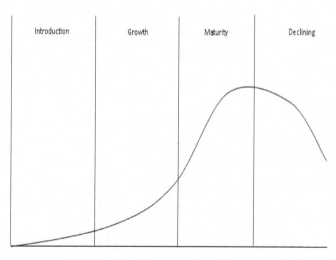

Shade in the phase your business is in.

Introduction Phase: Congratulations on starting your own business!

- Tell everyone you know about your product.
- Complete the Business Plan Template to make sure you are advertising to the right people.
- Ask other business owners how they kept their businesses running in the beginning.

Growth Phase: This is one of the most exciting parts of running your own business; all of your hard work is paying off!

- Increase the quality of your products.
- Reduce costs by buying the materials or ingredients you need to make your product in bulk or at a better price.
- Ask your customers for testimonials about your product or service to use in advertisements.

Maturity Phase: This means that your business is well-accepted and liked by your customers. Be careful that you don't get lazy.

- Complete the Business Plan Template to keep yourself focused on your original dreams for the business.
- Survey your customers to make sure that you are offering a product or service they want.
- Expand your product or service to include more options (e.g., new colors, sizes, location).

Declining Phase: As scary as this phase sounds, don't give up! There is plenty you can do to get your business going again! Here are some steps you should consider:

- <u>Ask your customers about your product or service and what could be changed to better meet their needs.</u>
- <u>Advertise your business in new places to reach a new group of customers.</u>

Future Plans

This product or service is currently in the _____ stage of the Product Life Cycle.

In order to grow or keep the business strong, we will do the following in the next three months:

1._____

2._____

3._____

Ask two friends or family members if they know of anything like your product or business that already exists. Record the results below. Alternately search the internet using search terms that describe your business!

1. Name of other business	_____
2. What they sell	_____
3. How much do they sell it for?	_____

1. Name of other business	_____
2. What they sell	_____
3. How much do they sell it for?	_____

Now that you know what else is out there, you can show how your product is better or different! This is called *differentiation*.

How My Business is Different
(circle adjectives below or add your own!)

cheaper   lasts longer   faster

tastes better   easier to use

better ingredients or materials   convenient

customizable   made locally

_____

_____

Differentiation Statements

For each business that offers something like yours, write a sentence that includes the following:

While (name of other business) does sell (what they sell) that is similar to (Company Name)'s (name of product/service you sell), our product/service is (circled adjectives).

Differentiation Statements

_____

_____

_____

_____

_____

_____

_____

_____

_____

_____

_____

_____

Customer Appreciation and Feedback

Cut out the sheets below (or make your own) to give to your most loyal customers. If they return them in two weeks, they can get a 10 percent off coupon on their next purchase from you!

THANK YOU!

You have been selected as one of _____'s best customers! Please write down how you feel about my business below. If you return this sheet in two weeks, you can redeem it for **10%** off your next purchase coupon!

Name: _____ Age: _____

_____
_____
_____
_____
_____

THANK YOU!

You have been selected as one of _____'s best customers! Please write down how you feel about my business below. If you return this sheet in two weeks, you can redeem it for **10%** off your next purchase coupon!

Name: _____ Age: _____

_____
_____
_____
_____
_____

Customer Feedback

Name: _____ Age: _____

_____

_____

Name: _____ Age: _____

_____

_____

PRICE

List all the steps you need to make your product. Then, write down the materials you'll need to complete each step and how much those materials will cost.

To-Do	Materials Needed	Cost of Materials
1.		
2.		
3.		
4.		
5.		
6.		
7.		
8.		
9.		
10.		
11.		
12.		
13.		
14.		
15.		
16.		
17.		
18.		
19.		

Next, add all the numbers in the "Cost of Materials" columns and write the sum below:

Total Cost of Materials: _____

How many products/services can you create with those materials?

Total Number of Products/Services:_____

Divide the total cost of materials by the total number of products/services. This is often called the Cost of Goods Sold, which means how much money you have to spend to make one product or service you can sell.

Cost Per Product/Service:_____

How much did the other businesses from the Product Research section charge for their products?

Business #1:_____ Price of Product:_____

Business #2:_____ Price of Product:_____

Business #3:_____ Price of Product:_____

How much are you going to charge for your product or service? Make sure that it is a larger amount than the Cost Per Product/Service. You can use the prices of other businesses like yours to decide what would be too high or whether you want to charge less than your competitors.

Pricing
Per Product/Service: $_____

PACKAGING

Do you remember the 5 adjectives that you wrote out about your product? Copy them down again here and use them as inspiration to design your packaging!

My product is: 1. _____ 2. _____

3. _____ 4. _____ 5. _____

Describe or color in the colors used for your packaging (try to stick to 3!).

A tagline is a catchy phrase to help customers remember what your product is about. For example, McDonald's uses the tagline: "I'm Lovin' It"™ and Trix Cereal uses "Silly Rabbit, Trix Are For Kids!"™

Write your own tagline below!

" _____ "

Draw or paste a picture of your logo:

Using the colors, logo, and tagline, draw or paste a picture of your packaging below!

Picture of Packaging

PLACE

There are so many places where people buy and sell things. For instance, if you were looking for a teddy bear to buy, you could go to a department store, a thrift store, a shopping mall, a garage sale, a craft store, a kids' toy shop, or a supermarket, just to name a few. It is really important to think about where your customers will be looking for a product like yours so you can make sure that you are selling your product in the right place. The best way to do that is to make sure that you know who your customers are and what kinds of things they like. The next few exercises will help you figure that out.

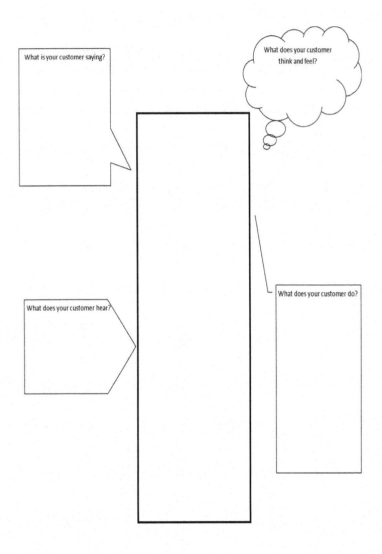

Draw a picture of what one of your customers would look like.

Target Market Description

Here at (Company Name), we are excited to serve our customers. Our target market is people that are (age), (gender), live in the (location) in a (type of house) and who typically have (spending money) to spend on products or services like ours.

Target Market Description

_____

_____

_____

_____

_____

Now that you know more about your customers, you can figure out where you should sell your product!

Where will your customers purchase your product?

Location
#1 Option:
_____
_____
_____
#2 Option:
_____
_____
_____
#3 Option:
_____
_____
_____

PROMOTION

You know what your business is about. You know what you are selling, how much it costs, how it will look, who would buy it, and where to sell. It might seem like everything is ready, but unless you promote your product, you might not be able to sell it. Promotion means spreading the word about your product and business and convincing people to try or buy it.

Below are the four main categories of promotion and some examples of how to use them. Circle the ones that you think would be best for your business. There are lots of ways to promote your business, so feel free to come up with your own.

Public Relations
> Press Release
> Facebook Page
> Newspaper Interview
> Community Contest

Advertising
> TV or Radio Commercial
> Newspaper or Magazine Ad
> Emails or Direct Letters
> Yearbook or Other Social Media Promotion

Sales Promotion
> Samples
> Coupons
> Buy-One-Get-One-Free Sale
> Discount Days for Students

Personal Selling
> Phone calls
> Door-to-Door
> Set up a Stand
> Talk to Friends and Family

Promotion Strategy

(Company's name) will promote itself using public relations through (examples of public relations strategies you will use). We will also do some personal selling by (examples of personal selling you will use) and advertise with (examples of advertising you will use). (Company's Name) will also do the sales promotions of (examples of sales promotions you will use).

Promotion Strategy

_____

_____

_____

_____

_____

_____

_____

_____

_____

_____

PROFIT

Profit Margin is the difference between how much money you made on each product or service and how much it cost you to make the product or service. You can find this by subtracting the "Cost Per Product" from the "Price per Product"

Price per Product - Cost Per Product = Profit Margin

$_____ - $_____ = $_____

How many products do you think you can sell in a week?

_____

Revenue is the total amount of money that you make by selling a product or service. To figure out how much money you are making, multiply the number of sales each week by the price you are charging.

Number of Products Sold x Price per Product = Total Revenue

_____ x $_____ = $_____

Total Profit is the amount of money that you get to keep! You can find it by taking the Total Revenue and subtracting the Total Cost of Materials (you found this number in the Price section).

Total Revenue – Total Cost of Materials = Total Profit

$_____ - $_____ = $_____

Profit Projections

Profit Margin: $_____

Sales in a Week: _____

Total Revenue: $_____

Total Profit: $_____

Congratulations! You now have all the information you need to make a fantastic business plan. Just transfer the information in the bold boxes from this worksheet to the boxes with the same titles in the Business Plan Template.

Business Plan Template

PLAN

> ### Mission Statement
>
> _____
>
> _____
>
> _____
>
> _____
>
> _____
>
> _____

PRODUCT

> ### Picture of Product or Service

Product Description

_____

_____

_____

_____

_____

Future Plans

This product or service is currently in the _____ stage of the Product Life Cycle.

In order to grow or keep the business strong, we will do the following in the next three months:

1._____

2._____

3._____

Differentiation Statements

_____
_____
_____
_____
_____
_____
_____
_____
_____
_____
_____
_____
_____

Customer Feedback

Name: _____ Age: _____

_____
_____

Name: _____ Age: _____

_____
_____

PRICE

Pricing

Per Product/Service: $_____

PACKAGING

Picture of Packaging

PLACE

Target Market Description

_____

_____

_____

_____

_____

Location

#1 Option:

_____

_____

_____

#2 Option:

_____

_____

_____

#3 Option:

_____

_____

_____

PROMOTION

Promotion Strategy

_____

_____

_____

_____

_____

_____

_____

_____

_____

PROFIT

Profit Projections

Profit Margin: $_____

Sales in a Week: _____

Total Revenue: $_____

Total Profit: $_____

Appendix 3: Savings Account Worksheet

When you receive your monthly bank statement, fill out this chart. The first line is given as an example.

Month	Starting Balance	Money Added (Deposited)	Interest Earned	Ending Balance
October	$50	$5	$0.20	$55.20

Appendix 4: $10 Challenge Worksheets

You and Your Business

Your
Name:_____

Name of Business: _____

What You are Selling:

_____
_____
_____
_____

Why People Want to Buy Your Product/Service:

_____
_____
_____
_____

Steps Needed to Make and Sell Your Product/Service:

To-Do	Materials Needed
1.	
2.	
3.	
4.	

5.	
6.	
7.	
8.	
9.	
10. Pay back the interest on the loan	Interest from loan

Making Money

Copy the Materials Needed column over from the "You and Your Business" worksheet. Then write down how much each material costs in the next column.

Materials Needed	Cost of Materials

Interest from loan	= $10 x .1 = $__

Next, add all numbers in the "Cost of Materials" column and write the sum below:

Total Cost of Materials: _____

(Remember: This should not be more than $11, which is the amount of the loan and the interest!)

How many products/services can you create with those materials?

Total Number of
Products/Services:_____

Divide the Total Cost of Materials by the Total Number of Products/Services and write the number below. This is often called the Cost of Goods Sold, which means how much money you have to spend to make one product or service you can sell.

Cost Per Product/Service:_____

How much are you going to charge for your product or service? Make sure that it is a larger amount than the number above.

Price Per Product/Service:_____

Profit Margin is the difference between how much money you made on each product or service and how much it cost you to make the product or service. You can find this by subtracting the "Cost Per Product/Service" from the "Price Per Product"

Profit Margin (Per Product/Service): _____

Sales: Use the chart below to keep track of how many products or services you sell each week

Week	Sales This Week (#)
Week 1	
Week 2	

Sales from Week 1 + Sales from Week 2 = Total Sales
____ + ____ = $_____

Revenue is the total amount of money that you make by selling a product or service. To figure out how much money you are making, multiply the number of sales each week by the price you are charging.

Week	Revenue This Week (Sales x Price)
Week 1	
Week 2	

Revenue from Week 1 + Revenue from Week 2 = Total Revenue

____ + ____ = $_____

To find how much money you get to keep from the business, subtract the "Total Cost of Materials" from "Total Revenue." This is your total profit!

Total Revenue – Total Cost of Materials = Total Profit

$_____ - $_____ = $_____

Appendix 5: Business Brainstorming Worksheet

Business Brainstorming Worksheet

Set Up: Set a timer for five minutes. During that time, the pencil can't leave the paper! There are no wrong answers, as long as you keep writing!

Top 3: What are your three favorite things to do? For each one, write what you enjoy most about that activity and what you would do to make it better.

1.   Activity:_____

_____
_____
_____
_____
_____

What I enjoy most:

_____
_____
_____
_____
_____
_____

If I could, I would change …

_____
_____
_____
_____
_____

2.   Activity:_____

_____

_____

_____

_____

_____

What I enjoy most:

_____

_____

_____

_____

_____

If I could, I would change ...

_____

_____

_____

_____

3.   Activity:_____

_____

_____

_____

_____

_____

What I enjoy most:

_____

_____

_____

_____

_____

If I could, I would change ...

_____

_____

_____

_____

_____

Tell Me About Your Day: Think about all the different things that happened today or yesterday.

What bothered you the most?

_____

_____

_____

_____

_____

_____

_____

_____

_____

_____

_____

What could you do to make it better?

_____

_____

_____

_____

_____

_____

ABOUT THE AUTHORS

Keith Greer is an aspiring entrepreneur with big dreams. He loves taxidermy, his pets, and (most of the time) his sister and brother.

Peter Greer is president and CEO of HOPE International and coauthor of *Entrepreneurship for Human Flourishing*, *Mission Drift*, *The Spiritual Danger of Doing Good*, *Mommy's Heart Went POP!*, and *The Poor Will Be Glad*. Visit him at www.peterkgreer.com, on Twitter (@peterkgreer), and on Facebook (facebook.com/peterkgreer).

Chloe Smiley is originally from Clarkston, Michigan, and is currently a student of entrepreneurship at Grove City College, where she has incorporated an e-commerce clothing nonprofit and for-profit children's healthcare company.

Keith and Peter Greer

HOPE

INTERNATIONAL

A portion of the proceeds from this book will go to support HOPE International, a Christ-centered microfinance organization serving those living in poverty through discipleship, savings groups, and small loans.

hopeinternational.org

Please share your stories of how you have used this book:

watchingseedsgrow.com